MAJESTI
Relax

COLORING
JOURNAL

PEACE LIKE A RIVER

MW00523064

BroadStreet
PUBLISHING

BroadStreet Publishing Group LLC
Racine, Wisconsin, USA
Broadstreetpublishing.com

MAJESTIC EXPRESSIONS

PEACE LIKE A RIVER

© 2016 by BroadStreet Publishing

ISBN 978-1-4245-4921-4

Cover design by Chris Garborg | garborgdesign.com
Compiled and edited by Michelle Winger | literallyprecise.com

Printed in the United States of America.

16 17 18 19 20 21 22   7 6 5 4 3 2 1

INTRODUCTION

· · · · · · · · · · · · · · · ·

There is plenty of research that shows coloring to be an effective stress reducer. Maybe you picked up this book because you've heard the hype and you're curious. Maybe you love to write. If you've been looking for a way to relax and express your creativity at the same time, here it is! Every time you open this coloring journal, you enter a stress-free zone.

While this is a great distraction from all you have going on, the best way to find lasting peace is to spend time with your Creator. As you fill the intricately designed illustrations and empty lines with your unique style of expression, dwell on the richness of God's Word, the faithfulness of his character, and the depth of his love for you.

BE INSPIRED!

This is the confidence that we have toward him, that if we ask anything according to his will he hears us.

1 John 5:14 ESV

GRACE AND PEACE BE YOURS IN ABUNDANCE.

1 PETER 1:2 NIV

_____

_____

_____

_____

_____

_____

_____

_____

_____

_____

_____

_____

_____

_____

_____

_____

TURN AWAY FROM EVIL AND DO GOOD.
SEARCH FOR PEACE, AND WORK TO MAINTAIN IT.
1 PETER 3:11 NLT

NOW MAY THE GOD OF PEACE MAKE YOU HOLY IN EVERY WAY,
AND MAY YOUR WHOLE SPIRIT AND SOUL AND BODY BE
KEPT BLAMELESS UNTIL OUR LORD JESUS CHRIST COMES AGAIN.

1 THESSALONIANS 5:23 NLT

MAY THE LORD OF PEACE HIMSELF GIVE YOU PEACE
AT ALL TIMES IN EVERY WAY.

2 THESSALONIANS 3:16 ESV

LET THE PEACE OF CHRIST RULE IN YOUR HEARTS, SINCE AS MEMBERS OF ONE BODY YOU WERE CALLED TO PEACE. AND BE THANKFUL.

COLOSSIANS 3:15 NIV

There Is No Fear In Love

1 John 4:18 NIV

HE CAME AND PREACHED PEACE TO YOU WHO WERE FAR AWAY
AND PEACE TO THOSE WHO WERE NEAR.

EPHESIANS 2:17 NIV

_____

_____

_____

_____

_____

_____

_____

_____

_____

_____

_____

_____

_____

_____

_____

_____

_____

_____

_____

_____

_____

_____

_____

_____

_____

_____

_____

_____

_____

_____

_____

_____

_____

WORK AT LIVING IN PEACE WITH EVERYONE, AND WORK AT LIVING A HOLY
LIFE, FOR THOSE WHO ARE NOT HOLY WILL NOT SEE THE LORD.

HEBREWS 12:14 NLT

YOU WILL KEEP IN PERFECT PEACE THOSE WHOSE MINDS ARE STEADFAST,
BECAUSE THEY TRUST IN YOU.

ISAIAH 26:3 NIV

_____

_____

_____

_____

_____

_____

_____

_____

_____

_____

_____

_____

_____

_____

_____

_____

_____

_____

_____

_____

_____

_____

_____

_____

_____

_____

_____

"THOUGH THE MOUNTAINS BE SHAKEN AND THE HILLS BE REMOVED, YET
MY UNFAILING LOVE FOR YOU WILL NOT BE SHAKEN NOR MY COVENANT OF
PEACE BE REMOVED," SAYS THE LORD, WHO HAS COMPASSION ON YOU.

ISAIAH 54:10 NIV

ALL YOUR CHILDREN WILL BE TAUGHT BY THE LORD,
AND GREAT WILL BE THEIR PEACE.

ISAIAH 54:13 NIV

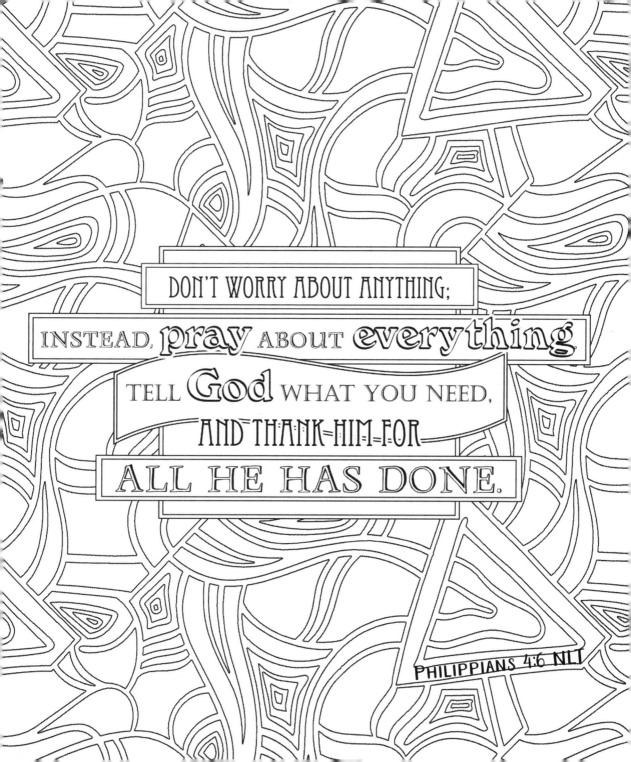

_____

_____

_____

_____

_____

_____

_____

_____

_____

_____

_____

_____

_____

_____

_____

_____

PEOPLE WHO WORK FOR PEACE IN A PEACEFUL WAY
PLANT A GOOD CROP OF RIGHT-LIVING.

JAMES 3:18 NCV

OBEY GOD AND BE AT PEACE WITH HIM; THIS IS THE WAY TO HAPPINESS.

JOB 22:21 NCV

_____

_____

_____

_____

_____

_____

_____

_____

_____

_____

_____

_____

_____

PEACE I LEAVE WITH YOU; MY PEACE I GIVE YOU.
I DO NOT GIVE TO YOU AS THE WORLD GIVES.
DO NOT LET YOUR HEARTS BE TROUBLED AND DO NOT BE AFRAID.

JOHN 14:27 NIV

I HAVE TOLD YOU ALL THIS SO THAT YOU MAY HAVE PEACE IN ME. HERE ON EARTH YOU WILL HAVE MANY TRIALS AND SORROWS. BUT TAKE HEART, BECAUSE I HAVE OVERCOME THE WORLD.

JOHN 16:33 NLT

PEACE BE WITH YOU.

JOHN 20:19 NCV

_____

_____

_____

_____

_____

_____

_____

_____

_____

_____

_____

_____

_____

_____

_____

MAY MERCY, PEACE, AND LOVE BE MULTIPLIED TO YOU.

JUDE 1:2 ESV

"I AM GOING TO SEND YOU WHAT MY FATHER HAS PROMISED: BUT STAY IN THE CITY UNTIL YOU HAVE BEEN CLOTHED WITH POWER FROM ON HIGH."

LUKE 24:49 NIV

_____

_____

_____

_____

_____

_____

_____

_____

_____

_____

_____

_____

_____

_____

_____

GOD BLESSES THOSE WHO WORK FOR PEACE,
FOR THEY WILL BE CALLED THE CHILDREN OF GOD.

MATTHEW 5:9 NLT

THE LORD lift up His countenance on you, And give you peace.

NUMBERS 6:26 NASB

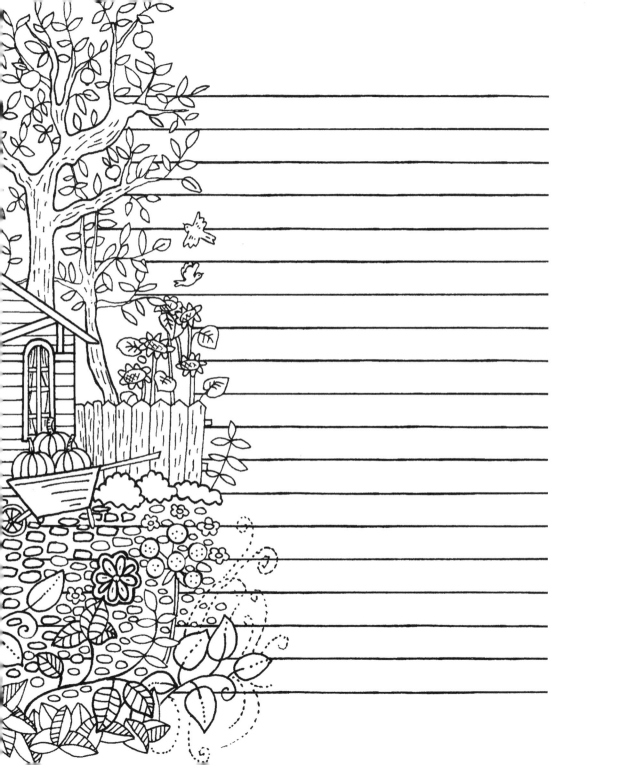

_____

_____

_____

_____

_____

_____

_____

_____

_____

_____

_____

_____

_____

_____

_____

_____

THOSE WHO PROMOTE PEACE HAVE JOY.

PROVERBS 12:20 NIV

GOD IS YOUR CONFIDENCE IN TIMES OF CRISIS,
KEEPING YOUR HEART AT REST IN EVERY SITUATION.
PROVERBS 3:26 TPT

_____

_____

_____

_____

_____

_____

_____

_____

_____

_____

_____

_____

_____

_____

_____

_____

_____

_____

_____

_____

_____

_____

_____

_____

_____

_____

_____

_____

_____

_____

_____

_____

_____

RELAX AND REST, BE CONFIDENT AND SERENE,
FOR THE LORD REWARDS FULLY THOSE WHO SIMPLY TRUST IN HIM.
PSALM 116:7 TPT

LORD, IT IS MUCH BETTER TO TRUST IN YOU TO SAVE ME
THAN TO PUT MY CONFIDENCE IN SOMEONE ELSE.
PSALM 118:8 TPT

THOSE WHO LOVE YOUR INSTRUCTIONS HAVE GREAT PEACE
AND DO NOT STUMBLE.

PSALM 119:165 NLT

_____

_____

_____

_____

_____

_____

_____

_____

_____

_____

_____

_____

_____

_____

_____

_____

_____

_____

_____

_____

_____

_____

_____

_____

_____

_____

_____

_____

_____

_____

_____

HE SENDS PEACE ACROSS YOUR NATION AND
SATISFIES YOUR HUNGER WITH THE FINEST WHEAT.

PSALM 147:14 NLT

Blessed is the one who trusts in the Lord, whose confidence is in him. They will be like a tree planted by the water that sends out its roots by the stream.

Jeremiah 17:7 NIV

_____

_____

_____

_____

_____

_____

_____

_____

_____

_____

_____

_____

_____

_____

_____

_____

_____

_____

YOU HAVE GIVEN ME THE SHIELD OF YOUR SALVATION, AND YOUR RIGHT
HAND SUPPORTED ME, AND YOUR GENTLENESS MADE ME GREAT.

PSALM 18:35 ESV

GUIDE ME IN YOUR TRUTH AND TEACH ME, FOR YOU ARE GOD MY SAVIOR,
AND MY HOPE IS IN YOU ALL DAY LONG.

PSALM 25:5 NIV

THE LORD GIVES STRENGTH TO HIS PEOPLE;
THE LORD BLESSES HIS PEOPLE WITH PEACE.

PSALM 29:11 NIV

DEPART FROM EVIL, AND DO GOOD; SEEK PEACE, AND PURSUE IT.

PSALM 34:14 NRSV

THE MEEK SHALL INHERIT THE LAND
AND DELIGHT THEMSELVES IN ABUNDANT PEACE.

PSALM 37:11 ESV

The one
who
always listens
to me will live
undisturbed in a heavenly peace.
Free from fear, confident and
courageous, you will rest
unafraid and sheltered
from the storms
of life.

Proverbs 1:33
TPT

BE STILL IN THE PRESENCE OF THE LORD,
AND WAIT PATIENTLY FOR HIM TO ACT.

PSALM 37:7 NLT

_____

_____

_____

_____

_____

_____

_____

_____

_____

_____

_____

_____

_____

_____

_____

_____

_____

I CAN LAY DOWN IN PEACE AND SLEEP COMES AT ONCE,
FOR NO MATTER WHAT HAPPENS, I WILL LIVE UNAFRAID!

PSALM 5:8 TPT

MY GOD IS CHANGELESS IN HIS LOVE FOR ME,
AND HE WILL COME AND HELP ME.
PSALM 59:10 TLB

MY PRAYER IS TO YOU, O LORD. AT AN ACCEPTABLE TIME,
O GOD, IN THE ABUNDANCE OF YOUR STEADFAST LOVE
ANSWER ME IN YOUR SAVING FAITHFULNESS.

PSALM 69:13 ESV

THE HUMBLE WILL SEE THEIR GOD AT WORK AND BE GLAD.
LET ALL WHO SEEK GOD'S HELP BE ENCOURAGED.

PSALM 69:32 NLT

The beautiful ways of God are a safe resting place for those who have integrity.

Proverbs 10:29 TPT

LET US PURSUE WHAT MAKES FOR PEACE AND FOR MUTUAL UPBUILDING.

ROMANS 14:19 ESV

SINCE WE ARE JUSTIFIED BY FAITH,
WE HAVE PEACE WITH GOD THROUGH OUR LORD JESUS CHRIST.

ROMANS 5:1 NRSV

THOSE WHO KNOW YOUR NAME TRUST IN YOU, FOR YOU, O LORD,
DO NOT ABANDON THOSE WHO SEARCH FOR YOU.

PSALM 9:10 NLT

YOU, O LORD, ARE A SHIELD ABOUT ME, MY GLORY,
AND THE ONE WHO LIFTS MY HEAD.

PSALM 3:3 NASB

_____

_____

_____

_____

_____

_____

_____

_____

_____

_____

_____

_____

_____

_____

_____

_____

ANYTHING IS POSSIBLE IF A PERSON BELIEVES.

MARK 9:23 NLT

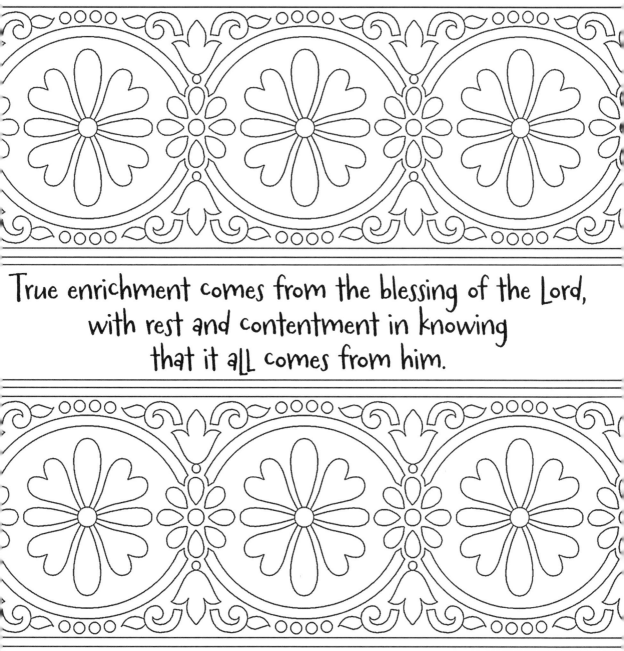

True enrichment comes from the blessing of the Lord,
with rest and contentment in knowing
that it all comes from him.

Proverbs 10:22 TPT

FROM HIS ABUNDANCE WE HAVE ALL RECEIVED
ONE GRACIOUS BLESSING AFTER ANOTHER.

JOHN 1:16 NLT

_____

_____

_____

_____

_____

_____

_____

_____

_____

_____

_____

_____

_____

_____

_____

_____

_____

COMMIT EVERYTHING YOU DO TO THE LORD. TRUST HIM,
AND HE WILL HELP YOU.

PSALM 37:5 NLT

I CAN DO EVERYTHING THROUGH CHRIST, WHO GIVES ME STRENGTH.

PHILIPPIANS 4:13 NLT

GOD IS NOT A GOD OF CONFUSION BUT OF PEACE.

1 CORINTHIANS 14:33 ESV

DO NOT LOSE THE COURAGE YOU HAD IN THE PAST,
WHICH HAS A GREAT REWARD. YOU MUST HOLD ON, SO YOU CAN DO
WHAT GOD WANTS AND RECEIVE WHAT HE HAS PROMISED.
HEBREWS 10:35-36 NCV

MAKE THE MOST OF EVERY OPPORTUNITY.

COLOSSIANS 4:5 NIV

_____

_____

_____

_____

_____

_____

_____

_____

_____

_____

_____

_____

_____

_____

_____

_____

YOU WILL LIGHT MY LAMP;
THE LORD MY GOD WILL ENLIGHTEN MY DARKNESS.

PSALM 18:28 NKJV

BEFORE THE MOUNTAINS WERE BROUGHT FORTH,
OR EVER YOU HAD FORMED THE EARTH AND THE WORLD,
FROM EVERLASTING TO EVERLASTING YOU ARE GOD.

PSALM 90:2 ESV

_____

_____

_____

_____

_____

_____

_____

_____

_____

_____

_____

_____

_____

_____

_____

SURELY GOODNESS AND MERCY SHALL FOLLOW ME ALL THE DAYS OF MY LIFE;
AND I WILL DWELL IN THE HOUSE OF THE LORD FOREVER.

PSALM 23:6 NKJV

WE FIX OUR EYES NOT ON WHAT IS SEEN, BUT ON WHAT IS UNSEEN,
SINCE WHAT IS SEEN IS TEMPORARY, BUT WHAT IS UNSEEN IS ETERNAL.
2 CORINTHIANS 4:18 NIV

In my trouble I cried to the Lord, and He answered me.

Psalm 120:1 NASB

_____

_____

_____

_____

_____

_____

_____

_____

_____

_____

_____

_____

THEREFORE I, THE PRISONER OF THE LORD, IMPLORE YOU TO WALK IN A MANNER WORTHY OF THE CALLING WITH WHICH YOU HAVE BEEN CALLED, WITH ALL HUMILITY AND GENTLENESS, WITH PATIENCE, SHOWING TOLERANCE FOR ONE ANOTHER IN LOVE, BEING DILIGENT TO PRESERVE THE UNITY OF THE SPIRIT IN THE BOND OF PEACE.

EPHESIANS 4:1-3 NASB

"PEACE BE WITH YOU! AS THE FATHER HAS SENT ME, I AM SENDING YOU."

JOHN 20:21 NIV

_____

_____

_____

_____

_____

_____

_____

_____

_____

_____

_____

_____

_____

_____

THE WISDOM THAT COMES FROM GOD IS FIRST OF ALL PURE,
THEN PEACEFUL, GENTLE, AND EASY TO PLEASE.
THIS WISDOM IS ALWAYS READY TO HELP THOSE WHO ARE TROUBLED
AND TO DO GOOD FOR OTHERS. IT IS ALWAYS FAIR AND HONEST.

JAMES 3:17 NCV

TASTE AND SEE THAT THE LORD IS GOOD;
BLESSED IS THE ONE WHO TAKES REFUGE IN HIM!

PSALM 34:8 NIV

_____

_____

_____

_____

_____

_____

_____

_____

_____

_____

_____

_____

_____

_____

_____

_____

_____

THE LORD HEARS HIS PEOPLE WHEN THEY CALL TO HIM FOR HELP.
HE RESCUES THEM FROM ALL THEIR TROUBLES.

PSALM 34:17 NLT

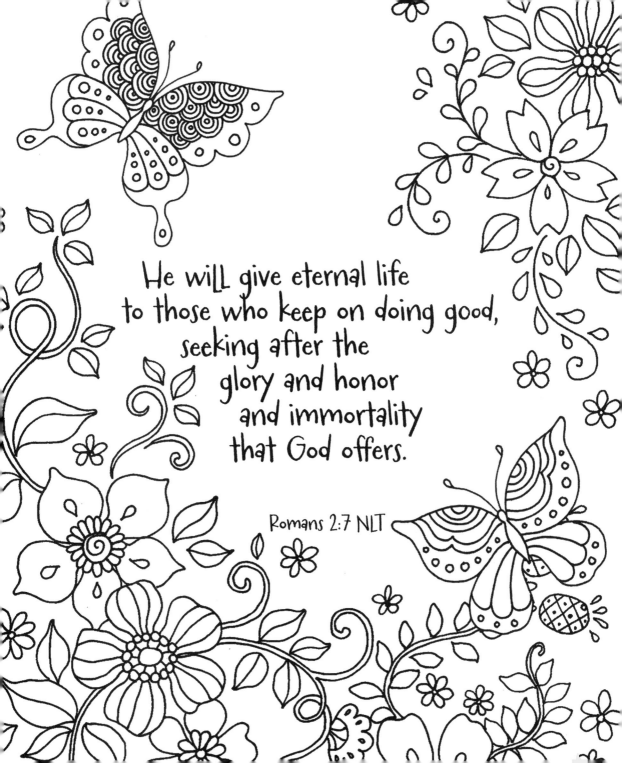

He will give eternal life
to those who keep on doing good,
seeking after the
glory and honor
and immortality
that God offers.

Romans 2:7 NLT

BECAUSE YOU ARE CLOSE TO ME AND ALWAYS AVAILABLE,
MY CONFIDENCE WILL NEVER BE SHAKEN,
FOR I EXPERIENCE YOUR WRAP-AROUND PRESENCE EVERY MOMENT.
PSALM 16:8 TPT

_____

_____

_____

_____

_____

_____

_____

_____

_____

_____

_____

_____

_____

_____

_____

_____

_____

_____

_____

_____

_____

_____

_____

_____

_____

_____

_____

_____

_____

_____

THE FAITHFUL LOVERS OF GOD WILL INHERIT THE EARTH
AND ENJOY EVERY PROMISE OF GOD'S CARE, DWELLING IN PEACE FOREVER.

PSALM 37:29 TPT

WISDOM OPENS YOUR HEART TO RECEIVE WISE COUNSEL.

PROVERBS 13:10 TPT